CLASSIFIED

SECRETS YOU'RE NOT SUPPOSED TO KNOW

CONSPIRACIES

Who's Hiding What?

Ellis Roxburgh

LUCENT PRESS

Published in 2019 by
Lucent Press, an Imprint of Greenhaven Publishing, LLC
353 3rd Avenue
Suite 255
New York, NY 10010

For Brown Bear Books Ltd:
Managing Editor: Tim Cooke
Designer: Lynne Lennon
Children's Publisher: Anne O'Daly
Design Manager: Keith Davis
Editorial Director: Lindsey Lowe
Picture Manager: Sophie Mortimer

Picture Credits
t=top, c=center, b=bottom, l=left, r=right
Interior: AP: 11; Breitbart News: 45; CNN: 41; Getty Images: AFP, 12, Boston Globe/Aram Bagnosian, 42, Washington Post/Bill O'Leary, 40; Library of Congress: 10; NASA: 33, 34; Public Domain: Alexisrael, 25, Paddy Briggs, 35, Dallas Morning News/Walt Cisco, 1, 23, LBJ Library/Cecil Stoughton, 31, National Numismatic Collection/National Museum of American History, 20, Raso 43, State of Hawaii Department of Health, 36, Walters Art Museum, 9, whitehouse.org, 5br; Reuters: 7, Luke MacGregor, 26; Robert Hunt Library: 16, 17, 18; Shutterstock: J. Bicking, 44, Felipe Caparros, 29, dugdax, 15, Everett Historical, 19, 27, Gorodenkoff, 28, Hadrian, 39, Dan Howell, 24, Jat306, 32, Kzenon, 37, Evan Meyer, 21, Jaroslav Moravcik, 4, Paper Cat, 5t, Jeremy Reddington, 13; TopFoto: Fortean, 8.
Front Cover: (background) Adisa/Shutterstock.com; (foreground) Richard Peterson/Shutterstock.com.

Brown Bear Books has made every attempt to contact the copyright holder.
If anyone has any information please contact licensing@brownbearbooks.co.uk

Cataloging-in-Publication Data

Names: Roxburgh, Ellis.
Title: Conspiracies: who's hiding what? / Ellis Roxburgh.
Description: New York : Lucent Press, 2019. | Series: Classified: secrets you're not supposed to know | Includes glossary and index.
Identifiers: ISBN 9781534564350 (pbk.) | ISBN 9781534564336 (library bound)
Subjects: LCSH: Conspiracy theories--Juvenile literature. | Conspiracies--Juvenile literature.
Classification: LCC HV6275.R69 2019 | DDC 001.9--dc23
Manufactured in the United States of America

CPSIA Compliance Information: Batch #BS18KL
For further information contact Rosen Publishing, New York, New York at 1-800-237-9932

CONTENTS

PLOTTING IN SECRET

Some people believe the world is subject to secret plots and hidden influences. That makes them reluctant to trust the official version of suspicious events.

A **conspiracy** is a secret plan by a group of people to do something unlawful or harmful. There have been many conspiracies throughout history, and others may still be taking place. However, not all alleged conspiracies are proven to exist. These are generally described as "**conspiracy theories**." Conspiracy theories are difficult to either prove or disprove.

Conspiracies and conspiracy theories have existed since ancient times. For example, some historians claim the pharaoh Tutankhamun was murdered by plotters to put a rival on the Egyptian throne.

>> **Boy King** The pharaoh Tutankhamun died in mysterious circumstances in around 1323 BC, aged just 18 years old.

>> Wall Street Bankers have been accused of working together to keep banking profits high.

MODERN CONSPIRACIES

In the 21st century, conspiracies have been uncovered in politics and business. After his election in 2016, U.S. president Donald J. Trump said that the media conspired against him. Trump's opponents said that he owed his victory partly to a conspiracy between his supporters and Russian computer **hackers**. The story has brought the idea of conspiracies back into public consciousness.

>> President Trump Trump's election sparked new interest in conspiracies in the modern world.

DO CONSPIRACIES EXIST?

Although many conspiracy theories seem highly unlikely, it is clear that real conspiracies have taken place in history and are probably still taking place today.

A reminder of the existence of conspiracies came in the 2016 U.S. presidential election. Hackers released thousands of personal emails relating to the Democratic candidate, Hillary Clinton. Clinton and her party alleged that the leak was the result of a conspiracy that involved Russia. After the election, U.S. intelligence confirmed Russian involvement and began investigating the extent of the conspiracy. However, many people dismissed the existence of a conspiracy. This reflects one of the main challenges about any conspiracy. It can be difficult to tell which conspiracies are real and supported by evidence, and which are the results of overactive imaginations.

>> Defeated Did Hillary Clinton lose the 2016 presidential election because of a conspiracy?

FAST FACTS

DEFINITIONS

There are different types of conspiracies. In legal terms, the word can describe any plan by two or more people to commit a crime. In general use, however, the word generally describes a widespread plot to achieve a large-scale political or economic aim, such as overthrowing a government.

ALIEN LANDING

Some conspiracy theorists are convinced the US government is concealing evidence that aliens have landed on Earth. In 1947, witnesses in Roswell, New Mexico, reported seeing a "flying disk" crash in the desert. The government claimed the accident involved a weather balloon. However, leaked photographs later appeared to reveal an alien body undergoing medical examination. Supporters of the conspiracy theory believe the photographs are genuine, even though the authorities deny this. Most people dismiss the images as being fakes. They point out that the "alien" looks suspiciously like aliens in science fiction movies.

TOP SECRET

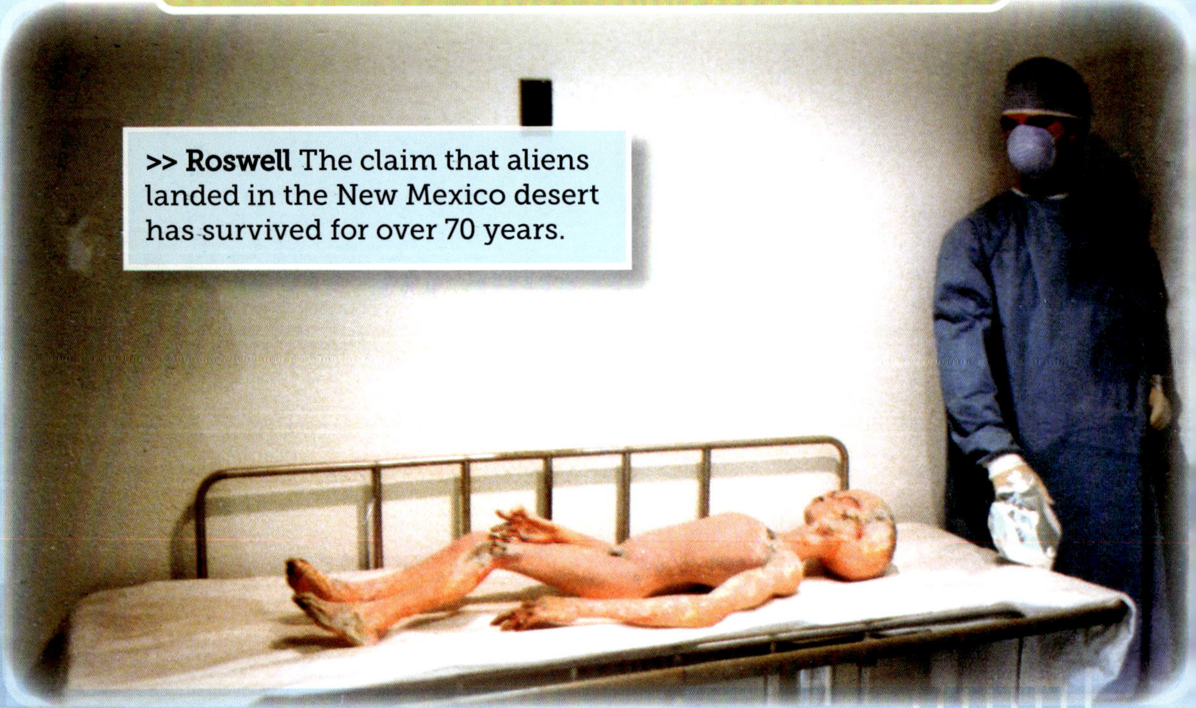

>> Roswell The claim that aliens landed in the New Mexico desert has survived for over 70 years.

KILL CAESAR!

There are many examples of real conspiracies in history. One of the most famous conspiracies happened in ancient Rome. In 44 BC, up to 60 Roman senators joined a secret plot to **assassinate** Julius Caesar. He had taken on the power to rule Rome as a dictator. The Liberatores, as they called themselves, gathered at each other's homes. They hatched a plan to prevent Caesar from destroying the Roman republic. They tricked Caesar into meeting with them and stabbed him to death on March 15.

>> Assassination
Roman senators murder the dictator Julius Caesar.

SECRET KNOWLEDGE

Some people believe that conspiracies are common among governments and the world's elite, but that they go largely unreported. They say these plots also involve the people whose job it would be to report them. They believe that powerful people always look after their own interests. However, this does not always take the form of a conspiracy. In the late 1800s, for example, U.S. businessmen formed **trusts** in which firms cooperated to keep prices artificially

>> Private Meeting President Warren G. Harding (second right) camps with industry leaders Henry Ford (left), Thomas A. Edison (second left), and Harvey Firestone (far right) in 1921.

high. When new laws outlawed trusts, conspiracy theorists believe that businesses continued to **collude** to keep their profits high—but now they did so by conspiring in secret.

Conspiracy theorists observe that both in the past and today, political parties and business have tended to include people from the same privileged social groups. They argue that many decisions or agreements that benefit those social groups may have been made secretly in private conversations. In the early 1900s, for example, U.S. political and business leaders began to meet informally at camps such as those organized by tire maker Harvey Firestone. Although the activity took place outside the formal structure of government, it is not usually seen as a conspiracy, as it was not illegal.

WATERGATE

One powerful tool against conspiracies is the growth of an investigational media. In 1972, two reporters from the *Washington Post* began to investigate a burglary at an office of the Democratic Party at the Watergate Hotel in Washington, D.C. The reporters, Carl Bernstein and Robert Woodward, uncovered a plot that had been authorized by senior figures in the Republican government. President Richard M. Nixon resigned in 1974 when it became clear that he had been trying to cover up the extent of the conspiracy.

FOR AND AGAINST

When defending his actions over the Watergate scandal, President Nixon later claimed, "When the president does it, that means it is not illegal." Nixon argued that his cover-up was in the best interests of the country. His critics denied this and prepared to **impeach** him. Nixon resigned from office before he could be impeached.

IRAN AND NICARAGUA

In 1986, another conspiracy was exposed. It linked the Republican government of then-president Ronald Reagan with the **fundamentalist** Islamic regime in Iran and right-wing terrorists trying to overthrow the government in Nicaragua. Under instructions from the U.S. government, U.S. military personnel were secretly selling arms to the Iranians, even though the trade was outlawed by an **embargo**. U.S. intelligence planned to use the money to fund the Contras, a right-wing militia in Nicaragua. Many senior members of the U.S. government were indicted and found guilty, though few were ever punished.

WHAT DO YOU THINK?

President Ronald Reagan and other presidents eventually pardoned nearly all US officials involved in the Iran-Contra plot. Those involved claimed that they were only following orders. Yet the actions involved in the plot were clearly illegal. Is it right that more senior people involved were not punished for their crimes?

>> Oliver North Marine officer Oliver North was not punished for his role in organizing the Iran-Contra Plot.

>> City of London
Workers in the financial center conspired to falsely influence money markets.

FINANCIAL CONSPIRACY

In the 21st century, conspiracies are sometimes associated with business. Large businesses have a lot of power, and some individuals try to take advantage of this. In London, UK, for example, a number of banks conspired to manipulate the rate at which banks loaned money to each other, the London Interbank Offered Rate (Libor). Officials from a range of banks agreed to quote inaccurate figures to make Libor rise or fall, so that the banks could increase their profits. The conspiracy was only revealed in 2012, after it had been going on for up to two decades. Such conspiracies encourage a widespread perception that large organizations such as banks operate in secret ways in order to preserve their own power and wealth, even at the cost of breaking the law and harming the interests of ordinary people.

CONSPIRACIES IN HISTORY

Conspiracies have existed for centuries. Their long existence makes many people today suspicious of those in positions of power.

One common factor in many conspiracies and conspiracy theories is religion. In a long period called the Reformation that began in the early 1500s, a new type of Christianity named Protestantism challenged the dominant influence of the Catholic Church in Europe. The bitter division between Catholics and Protestants led to a series of conspiracies and conspiracy theories. Protestants accused the Catholic Church and its head, the Pope, of plotting to overthrow the governments of Protestant nations.

In England, King Henry VIII made Protestantism the national religion in 1533. When his daughter, Mary Tudor, became queen in 1553, she restored Catholicism. Mary killed more than 300 Protestants for their beliefs. Mary died in 1558, and was succeeded by her half-sister, Queen Elizabeth I. Elizabeth brought back Protestantism as the official religion.

>> Reformation The German monk Martin Luther led protests against the Catholic Church in 1517.

FAST FACTS

MOTIVATION

In history, a common motive for conspiracies has been conflict between religions or between branches of the same religion. Political differences have also inspired conspiracies against opposing factions or parties. Economic conspiracies aim to make money through criminal activity, such as price-fixing or **insider trading.**

>> **Elizabeth I** As queen, Elizabeth brought back Protestantism to England and executed Catholics.

PLOTS IN ENGLAND

English Catholics plotted to overthrow Elizabeth and replace her with her Catholic relative, Mary Queen of Scots. Real conspiracies were discovered before they were carried out. In the Babington Plot of 1586, for example, Anthony Babington and other Catholics planned to help Mary escape from the castle where Elizabeth had her imprisoned. They planned to begin an uprising to overthrow Elizabeth. However, a coded letter from Babington to Mary was intercepted. The plot was revealed and stopped.

WHAT DO YOU THINK?

In some countries, distrust of Catholics lasted until quite recently. They resurfaced when John F. Kennedy became the first Catholic president of the United States in 1961. Some people suspect that Catholics must have a greater loyalty to the Pope than they do to the United States. Is there evidence that these kind of prejudices still exist?

Elizabeth had Mary executed in 1587, but Catholic conspiracies continued into the reign of James I, who came to the throne on the death of Elizabeth in 1603. James was the former king of Scotland, a Protestant country. In the Gunpowder Plot in 1605, a group of Catholics conspired to blow up the Houses of Parliament in order to kill James I and most of his government. A plotter named Guy Fawkes was found with gunpowder the night before the planned explosion. The plotters were caught and executed.

Suspicion of Catholics remained high. In 1678, an anti-Catholic named Titus Oates alleged the existence of a "Popish Plot" to kill King Charles II, backed up by letters apparently written by the plotters. Oates's accusations led to the execution of at least 22 Catholics before the plot was exposed as false.

>> Titus Oates Oates himself wrote the letters behind the Popish Plot.

ANTISEMITISM

>> Negative Caricature
Throughout European history, Jews have often been portrayed as ugly and greedy.

Other early conspiracy theories were related to Jews who lived in scattered communities throughout Europe. The fact that they were seen as outsiders with their own religion, language, and culture made them the target of **antisemitic** conspiracies and prejudice. Christians spread stories that it had been the Jews who had killed Jesus, not the Romans as the Bible stated. The Jews were also blamed for killing children to use their blood in religious rituals—an accusation known as the blood libel—and for poisoning wells to spread the **Black Death** in the Middle Ages.

One of the most famous antisemitic conspiracies was a document called Protocols of the Elders of Zion. It spread the myth of a secret, worldwide Jewish conspiracy. It led to riots in Russia, where it was made public in 1905. The document was later shown to be a fake. However, the idea of a worldwide Jewish conspiracy persisted for over 100 years.

DEATH OF LINCOLN

One of the most successful political conspiracies was that of Confederate sympathizers to kill Abraham Lincoln after the Civil War (1861–1865). Lincoln was shot by John Wilkes Booth on April 14, 1865, and died the next day. Scores of people were suspected of involvement in the plot, of whom eight were tried. Four were executed and four imprisoned. Those imprisoned included a stagehand who claimed that Booth had simply asked him to hold his horse.

TOP SECRET

>> Assassination
Lincoln was shot as he watched a play at the theater.

>> Hyperinflation This 500 million mark banknote was printed in Germany in the 1920s, when paper money lost all its value.

When Adolf Hitler rose to power in Germany in the 1920s, he argued that a conspiracy by Jewish bankers had caused German defeat in World War I and was responsible for high **inflation** and unemployment in Germany. A similar theory resurfaced almost a century later, in the 2010s, when social media alleged a secret takeover of the world economy by the Rothschilds, a Jewish banking family.

WORLD TAKEOVER

The alleged plot by the Rothschilds brought together two groups often accused of being involved in conspiracies: Jews and bankers. Other favorite suspects for global plots are business leaders, politicians, and international organizations, such as the United Nations. British conspiracy theorist, David Icke, believes such groups are a front for reptile-like aliens plotting to take over the world. Other groups accused of trying to establish a new world government are the Freemasons and the Illuminati.

FOR AND AGAINST

Many people believe the world's elite rule the world for their own benefit. There are various forums through which people allege this takes place. One is the private annual conference of the Bilderberg Group, featuring leading figures from politics, finance, industry, and the media. Another is the yearly encampment at Bohemian Grove in Monte Rio, California, for prominent American figures. Those who take part in such informal discussions argue that they are a normal part of the process of government.

The Freemasons are an organization based on medieval craft guilds. Their members are often prominent in society. The Illuminati were founded in Germany in 1776 to support limits on state power. Both the Freemasons and the Illuminati operated in the past in a secret way, and both operate beyond national boundaries. This makes them targets for conspiracy theorists worried about international takeover.

>> **Denver Airport** One conspiracy theory is that a secret city beneath Denver Airport is the capital of a secret world government.

CONSPIRACY THEORIES

A conspiracy theory is a way to explain events as the results of secret action by a group of people, such as governments, corporations, or criminal organizations.

The starting point of many people who believe in conspiracy theories—called conspiracy theorists—is that nothing is as it appears, particularly with regard to important events. Such events include the deaths of public figures, such as President John F. Kennedy, who was shot dead in 1963. They also include major historical events, such as the **Holocaust** in World War II and the moon landing in 1969. Despite evidence that is accepted by virtually every historian and member of the public, some conspiracy theorists insist that the Holocaust and the moon landing were faked.

One of the most notorious conspiracy theories is Holocaust denial. The Holocaust is the name given to the murder of six million Jews and many other victims by the Nazis in Germany during World War II. Every serious historian considers the Holocaust to be a documented historical event.

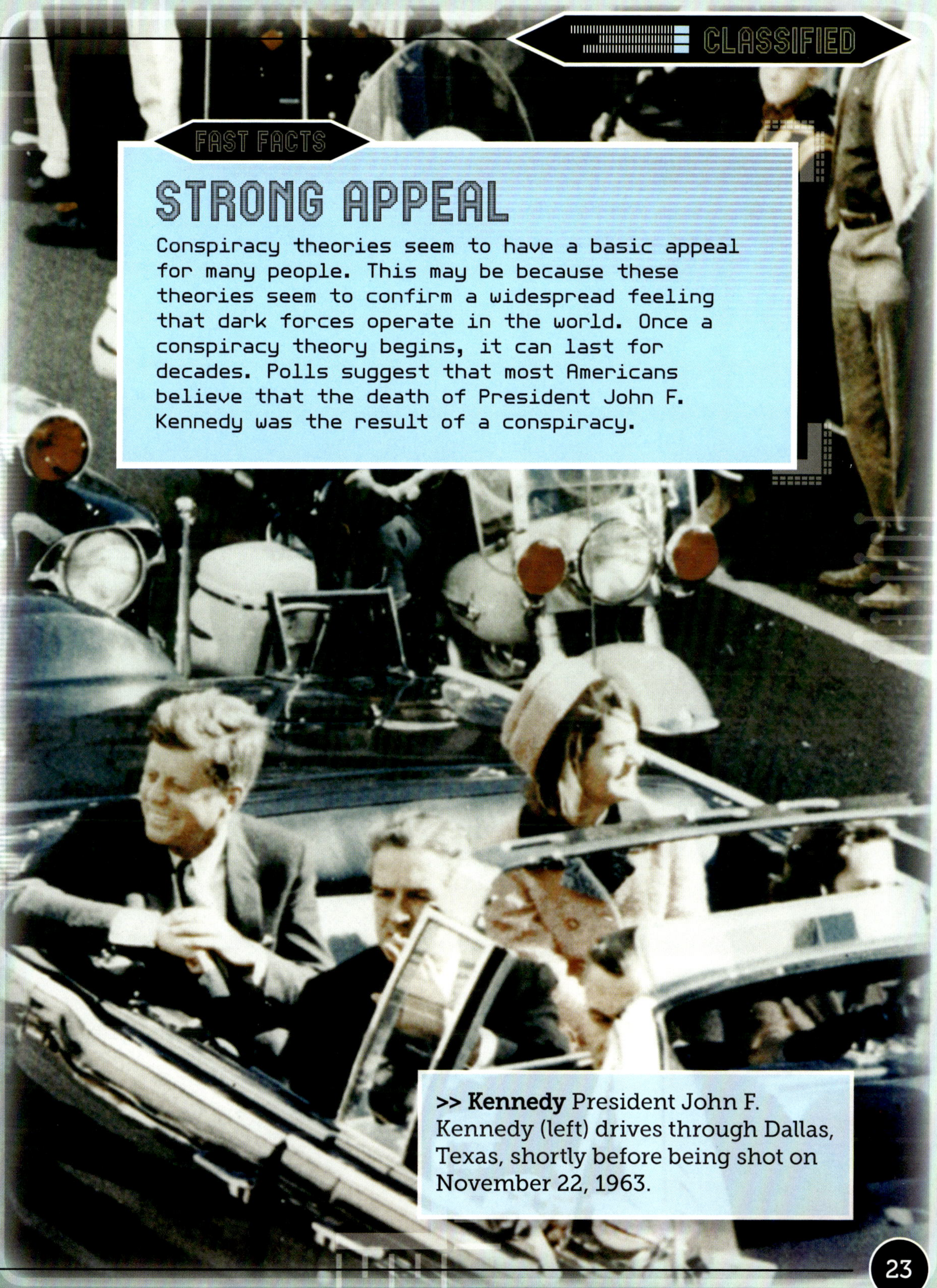

FAST FACTS

STRONG APPEAL

Conspiracy theories seem to have a basic appeal for many people. This may be because these theories seem to confirm a widespread feeling that dark forces operate in the world. Once a conspiracy theory begins, it can last for decades. Polls suggest that most Americans believe that the death of President John F. Kennedy was the result of a conspiracy.

>> **Kennedy** President John F. Kennedy (left) drives through Dallas, Texas, shortly before being shot on November 22, 1963.

There are thousands of Holocaust survivors, along with photographs and records of the people murdered. Despite this overwhelming evidence, a tiny minority of people deny that the Holocaust took place. They say a conspiracy made up the story to gain sympathy for Jewish people.

TERRORIST ATTACKS

Another historical event that has given rise to conspiracy theories is the 9/11 terrorist attacks of 2001. Hijacked airliners flew into the World Trade Center in New York City, the Pentagon in Washington, D.C., and a field in Pennsylvania, killing 2,977 people.

>> **Twin Towers** Both towers of the World Trade Center collapsed after they were struck by airplanes on September 11, 2001.

WHAT DO YOU THINK?

On December 14, 2012, Adam Lanza shot and killed 26 people at Sandy Hook Elementary School in Newtown, Connecticut. Lanza then shot himself. A number of conspiracy theories soon emerged. One was that the U.S. government had staged the atrocity to promote gun control. Another denied that the incident had happened at all. There was no evidence for this claim, which outraged citizens in Sandy Hook. Should people's right to promote such conspiracy theories be limited?

>> **Victims** Candles form a memorial to the children and staff killed in the Sandy Hook shootings.

The U.S. government blamed the attacks on the al-Qaeda Islamic group, which claimed responsibility. However, some people insist that the attacks were part of a conspiracy. They claim that the buildings were rigged with explosives to blow up from inside, so that they could collapse. They claim that the U.S. government was trying to manufacture a reason to go to war with Islamic countries. The conspiracy theory became very popular. In 2016, a survey suggested that more than half of Americans believed the government was concealing information about the events of 9/11.

ALTERNATIVE VIEWS

Most uses of the term "conspiracy theory" are negative. The term is used to criticize people who refuse to believe simple explanations of events and who believe that the world is controlled by hidden influences. Most people reject such suspicions. They tend to trust the authorities and also to trust explanations of events based on widely accepted evidence. This has the effect of opening a gap in the way the general public and conspiracy theorists view historical events.

TOP SECRET

In 1998, British doctor Andrew Wakefield (right) claimed that the **vaccine** against measles, mumps, and rubella (MMR) caused autism. The rate of vaccination fell, and the incidence of the diseases rose. In 2010, the journal that published the original claim said that Wakefield had made up his evidence. He lost his medical license, but he still promotes his theory of a medical conspiracy to hide the truth about autism.

>> Pearl Harbor Conspiracy theorists believe the U.S. government had prior warning of the Japanese attack on Pearl Harbor in 1941.

Conspiracists believe that the majority of people have been **brainwashed** into accepting inaccurate explanations of events. A common quality of conspiracy theorists is their dismissal of any new evidence as a sign of a conspiracy in action. That attitude makes it almost impossible to persuade an extreme conspiracy theorist to change their mind through rational argument.

CIRCULATING THEORIES

Conspiracy theories became particularly popular in the late 1900s. One reason for this was the rise of the Internet. The Internet not only gave researchers access to international resources and information. It also gave them a platform for their theories. Because the Internet is not subject to critical review like academic articles or books by established publishers, people were free to publish their ideas with weak or even no evidence. This helped to increase the number of conspiracy theories in circulation.

Above all, the Internet allowed the small number of people who believed in conspiracies to contact like-minded people. This led to the creation of a community that distrusts official versions of events and circulates its own. This itself confirms a common belief among conspiracy theorists that all conspiracies are linked. For such people, conspiracy theories merely reflect the reality of a sinister and secret world.

CLIMATE CHANGE

The election of Donald Trump as U.S. president in 2016 gave conspiracy theories even more publicity. Trump had previously questioned whether human activity was really causing global warming. He called **climate change** a hoax.

>> Internet Café The Internet has made conspiracy theories easier to propose—but also easier to investigate and challenge.

In June 2017, Trump announced his decision to pull the United States out of an international deal on climate change signed by 195 parties in Paris in 2015. Conspiracy theories against climate change had had a direct influence on the real world.

FOR AND AGAINST

Evidence suggests the atmosphere is growing warmer, causing floods, droughts, and rising sea levels with disastrous results for communities around the world. The vast majority of experts believe this change is caused in part by human activity, such as releasing **greenhouse gases.** A much smaller group argues that the change is natural, and that blaming human activity is the result of a conspiracy among scientists, politicians, and environmentalists.

INVESTIGATING CONSPIRACIES

Conspiracies are difficult to investigate. By their nature, they are secret. People who plan real conspiracies go to great lengths to cover them up.

Illegal conspiracies, like other crimes, are usually investigated by law enforcement agencies and official bodies. After the shooting of John F. Kennedy, President Lyndon B. Johnson set up the Warren Commission to investigate who was behind the killing. The commission concluded that the official suspect, Lee Harvey Oswald, had acted alone and that there was no conspiracy. Serious investigations into conspiracies also come from investigative journalists, such as the *Washington Post* reporters who uncovered the Watergate Scandal. However, there is another sort of conspiracy investigation. These are carried out by amateur enthusiasts who suspect a conspiracy where no one else does or who reject official accounts of events. Amateur investigators have blamed Kennedy's death on at least 40 different conspiracies. They have named more than 80 possible assassins.

>> Report Chief Justice Earl Warren hands the report to President Lyndon B. Johnson.

FAST FACTS

OFFICIAL COMMISSION

The Warren Commission set up by President Johnson in 1963 found no evidence of a conspiracy in the killing of President Kennedy. In 1979, the U.S. House Select Committee on Assassinations suggested that two gunmen had been involved and that there had been a conspiracy. However, it did not say who had carried it out.

>> Files Amateur investigators often work for years to collect evidence that supports their theories.

RESEARCHING THEORIES

These unofficial researchers often attempt to find evidence of a conspiracy they suspect exists. They study official records, photographs, and videos for clues. However, one characteristic of conspiracy theorists is that they do not trust official accounts of events. They assume that evidence is inaccurate or has been altered. Sometimes they claim to see evidence in photographs and records that others cannot.

FOR AND AGAINST

Many conspiracy theorists distrust experts. They believe that academics, journalists, and others are part of an establishment that plays a part in covering up conspiracies. Yet experts argue that amateur investigators trying to investigate conspiracy theories are in danger of misinterpreting evidence because of a lack of knowledge or experience.

MOON LANDING

One example of this is the photographs of the moon landing sent back from the moon by Apollo 11 in 1969. Those who believe the landing was a hoax interpret shadows in the photographs as evidence that the images were taken in a studio under lights. They say that the flag appears to flutter, but the moon has no wind to move a flag. They suggest that famous images of the astronauts' footprints are so sharply defined that they must have been made in wet sand, whereas the lunar surface is dry.

>> **Moonwalk** Conspiracy theorists question the photographs of the 1969 moon landing.

Experts at the National Aeronautics and Space Administration (NASA) have explained these apparent **anomalies**. For example, they explained that the dust on the surface of the moon is so fine that it does create clear edges as seen in the photographs of the astronauts' footprints. Yet conspiracy theorists insist NASA is lying to cover up the conspiracy.

>> Footprint The impression left by an astronaut's boot in the moon dust is very sharp.

Faking the moon landings would have involved many thousands of people. NASA employees, contractors, politicians, and people in the media would all have to be involved. None of the people involved have come forward to confirm that the landings were staged.

DEATH OF A PRINCESS

Another event that has been widely investigated is the death of Diana, Princess of Wales, in Paris on August 31, 1997. Diana, her boyfriend Dodi al-Fayed, and the driver died when their car crashed in an underpass. The official explanation was that the driver was drunk and lost control as he tried to escape **paparazzi** trying to photograph the couple.

However, Dodi's father, Mohamed al-Fayed, claimed that British intelligence had staged the accident. He said they wanted to cover up the fact that Diana was pregnant. He also claimed the British wanted to prevent the possibility that his son, an Egyptian, might marry Diana and become stepfather to the future British king, Prince William. Another theory said that the driver worked for the French secret services.

WHAT DO YOU THINK?

People who believe in conspiracy theories often reject evidence that a conspiracy does not exist. The more evidence is presented to disprove a conspiracy, the more they believe that the conspirators are hiding their actions. Does that mean that conspiracy theories can never be disproved?

>> Princess Diana's Funeral Some people claim British secret services killed Princess Diana in a car crash in 1997.

There was some evidence that Diana herself had suggested that she would be killed by the British "establishment" because she was more popular than the royal family. After Diana's death, these theories gained momentum, thanks partly to the claims of Mohamed al-Fayed, supported by some UK newspapers. In 2004, the Metropolitan Police in London opened Operation Paget. This official investigation studied 175 conspiracy theories about the accident. In 2006, the investigation reported that there was no evidence that any of them were true. However, that did not prevent amateur investigators from continuing to come up with more "evidence" about the causes of the accident.

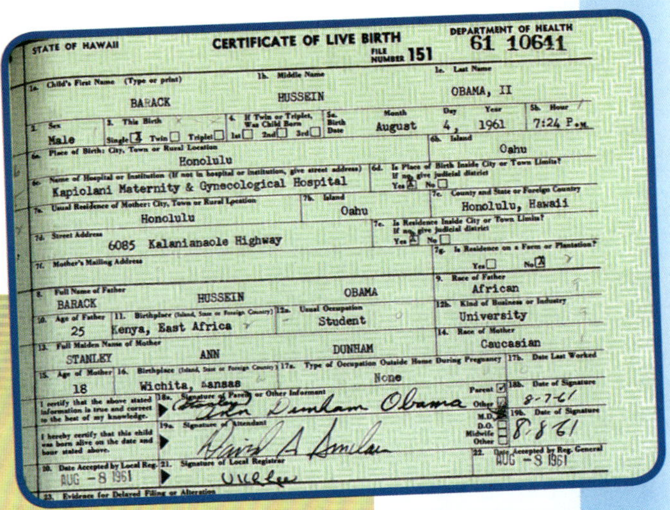
STATE OF HAWAII
CERTIFICATE OF LIVE BIRTH
FILE NUMBER 151
DEPARTMENT OF HEALTH
61 10641
Child's First Name (Type or print): BARACK
Middle Name: HUSSEIN
Last Name: OBAMA, II
Sex: Male
This Birth: Single
Birth Date: August 4, 1961
Hour: 7:24 P.M.
Place of Birth: City, Town or Rural Location: Honolulu
Island: Oahu
Name of Hospital or Institution: Kapiolani Maternity & Gynecological Hospital
Usual Residence of Mother: City, Town or Rural Location: Honolulu
Island: Oahu
County and State or Foreign Country: Honolulu, Hawaii
Street Address: 6085 Kalanianaole Highway
Full Name of Father: BARACK HUSSEIN OBAMA
Race of Father: African
Age of Father: 25
Birthplace: Kenya, East Africa
Usual Occupation: Student
Kind of Business or Industry: University
Full Maiden Name of Mother: STANLEY ANN DUNHAM
Race of Mother: Caucasian
Age of Mother: 18
Birthplace: Wichita, Kansas
Type of Occupation Outside Home During Pregnancy: None
Date of Signature: 8-7-61
Date of Signature: 8-8-61
Date Accepted by Local Reg.: AUG - 8 1961
Date Accepted by Reg. General: AUG - 8 1961

TOP SECRET

One of the most notorious recent conspiracy theories was the so-called "birther" conspiracy. This argued that Barack Obama was not born in the United States, so could not be U.S. president. One of the main supporters of the theory was Donald Trump. Even after Obama published his birth certificate (above), many Republicans still disbelieved his U.S. citizenship. Others claimed that Obama was a Muslim, which has been disproved.

DENTAL HEALTH CONSPIRACY

Allegations about conspiracies tend to change. This makes it harder to investigate them. In the 1940s and 1950s, for example, many states began adding the chemical fluoride to drinking water supplies. Scientists found that the chemical helped prevent cavities in teeth. During the 1940s and 1950s, right-wing groups claimed that the fluoridation of water was part of a communist plot to weaken the mental capacity of U.S. children.

By the 1980s, the theory had evolved. Now the "criminal" was the U.S. government itself. Critics said the government was adding fluoride to water to make people easier to control. In the early 2000s, the theory changed again. Critics argued that the people behind the plot were manufacturers of fluoride, who simply wanted to sell more fluoride.

>> **Fluoride** Fluoride is included in many popular toothpastes to help prevent cavities.

FAKE NEWS

"Fake news" became a familiar phrase in 2017. It originated during the presidential election campaign in 2016 between Donald Trump for the Republicans and Hillary Clinton for the Democrats.

The term became widespread after the election of Donald Trump as the 45th president. After taking office, Trump often used the label to criticize traditional media outlets, including newspapers such as *The New York Times* and TV stations such as CNN. Trump argued that such media did not want to describe events accurately. He said that they were more concerned with reporting things that reflected badly on him and his presidency.

The media maintained that they were reporting facts and public opinion as they had always done—but the president did not like what they were reporting. When the Trump administration claimed that the crowd for his inauguration was the biggest in history, for example, the media published photographs showing that this was not the case. Pictures of Barack Obama's inauguration showed more people on the Mall in Washington, D.C. A White House spokesperson said that the administration was providing "alternative facts." She suggested that these facts were just as valid as the facts presented by the press.

>> **MSM** Donald Trump and his supporters often dismiss what they call the mainstream media—MSM.

FAST FACTS

CHANGING MEANINGS

In the first six months of his presidency, Donald Trump tweeted about "fake news" 73 times. Observers noted that his use of the phrase changed. It originally referred to a fictional story. Later, he used it to describe predictions that did not come true. Finally, he used it to describe opinions with which he did not agree.

>> Alternative Facts
President Trump's team dismissed pictures showing empty areas at his inauguration.

The origins of fake news lie in social media, such as Facebook or Twitter. News stories reported on such platforms have no filter. There is no authority, such as the editors on traditional newspapers who evaluate whether a story stands up to **scrutiny**. Stories from unknown sources can be circulated so widely that they end up being reported in the traditional media as "news."

NEWS ON SOCIAL MEDIA

Academics who studied the 2016 presidential election campaign found that over 60 percent of U.S. adults got at least some of their news from social media, and that people who saw fake news stories tended to believe them. Such stories included a claim that an FBI agent suspected of leaking Hillary Clinton's emails had killed himself.

Most fake news stories were tilted in favor of Donald Trump, by a ratio of nearly 3 to 1. However, Republicans and Democrats were all more likely to believe stories that reflected their own political views. In addition, it was widely reported that people were becoming less trusting of established daily newspapers and TV networks.

WHY MAKE FAKE NEWS?

Fake news stories were deliberately created to be misleading. Some came from satirical websites that have been creating humorous fictional news stories for many years. Others were created by people who had political sympathies for one or other of the candidates. A vast number of stories were created by people simply in order to make money.

WHAT DO YOU THINK?

In the past, people got their news from newspapers and TV and radio news. These media are being challenged by online news outlets. More people get their news from sources such as social media. Does it matter that these new media sources often lack the fact-checking apparatus and editorial **accountability** of the traditional news media?

>> **Viewers** watch TV in a diner. Lara Trump's news show is an attempt to bypass mainstream TV channels.

FOR AND AGAINST

In August 2017, Donald Trump's daughter-in-law, Lara Trump, hosted the first edition of the Real News Show. The show was broadcast on the president's Facebook page. The White House claimed the show was a way to avoid **biased** reporting by the mainstream news. The president's opponents responded that it was simply a way to try to avoid media scrutiny of the government's record.

SPREADING FAKE NEWS

Most fake news stories originally appear on websites with names similar to those of legitimate news organizations. The sites have names such as denverguardian.com or USAToday.com.co. Journalists who investigated these fake-news websites found that more than 100 sites that generated fake news during the 2016 election campaign were run by teenagers from the town of Veles in Macedonia, in southeastern Europe. In the United States, multiple fake news sites were owned by a company named Disinfomedia.

These sites generated stories that would appear on social media as "click bait." The stories were often scandalous and quirky. They were designed to encourage social media users to click and link to the websites where they could read the stories. The more readers visited the websites, the more revenue the sites could attract from advertisers. Researchers reported that people who saw fake news stories were more likely to remember them than they were to remember real news stories, possibly because the stories contained more striking elements than real stories.

>> **Macedonia** Teens in Veles made up hundreds of fake news stories in order to earn money.

After his election, Trump continued to denounce the mainstream media. He condemned as fake news investigations into links between his electoral team and Russian organizations, which the FBI reported had used its own fake news stories to influence the presidential election. He used Twitter to give accounts of events that contradicted those in the press.

>> Protest Opponents of Donald Trump's criticism of climate change legislation use the president's "fake news" accusation against him.

WHO TO TRUST?

In October 2017, a public opinion poll found that 46 percent of Americans believed that major news organizations made up critical stories about President Donald Trump. That was particularly true among Republicans, of whom 76 percent believed stories were made up. Democrats were more likely to believe such reports. The poll was a reminder that an atmosphere of mistrust surrounded the activities of the traditional media.

TOP SECRET

POLITICIZED MEDIA

Meanwhile, many websites and message boards in the United States circulated stories favorable to the new president. They included conservative news sites such as Breitbart. Other sites were less reliable, including the anarchistic message board 4chan, where posters are anonymous, and "alt-right" sites that circulate misleading stories to report their own right-wing political agenda. It seems that in the future people may need to find out about a story's origins to judge whether it reflects an objective truth, a subjective opinion—or is nothing but "fake news."

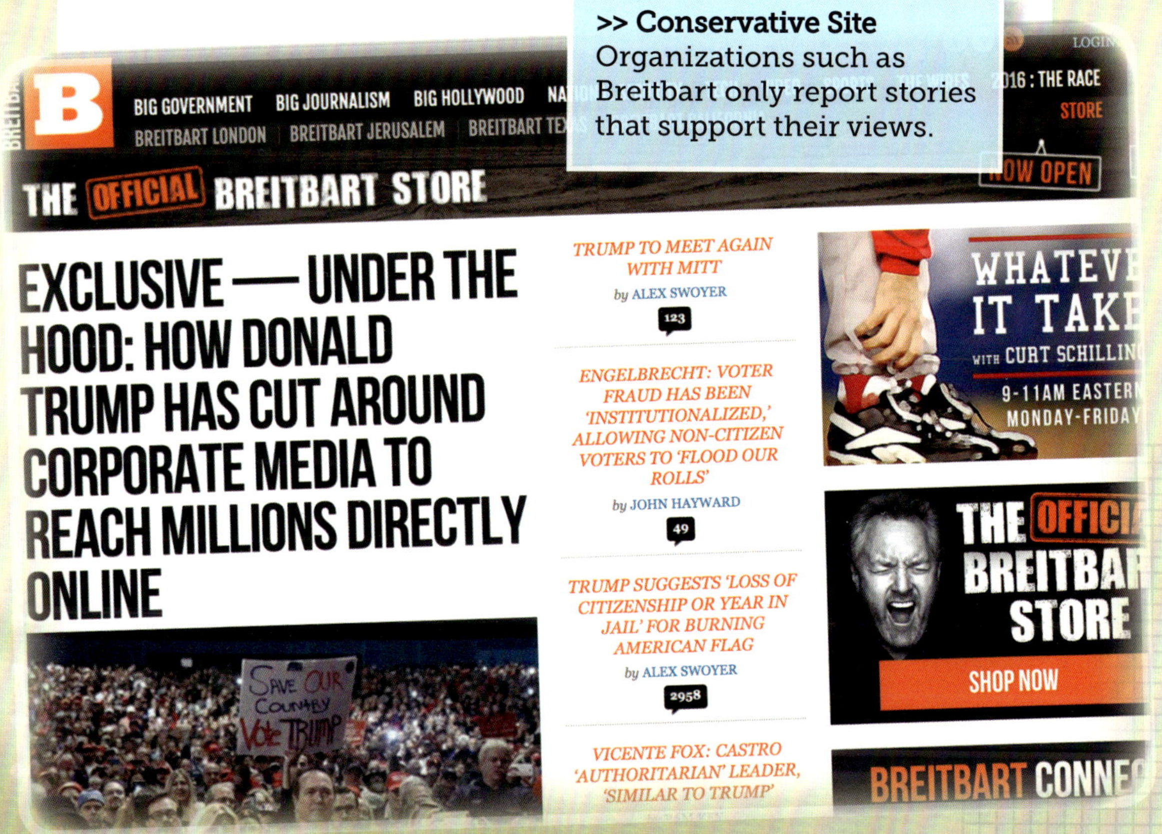

>> Conservative Site
Organizations such as Breitbart only report stories that support their views.

GLOSSARY

accountability The requirement to give justifiable reasons for a course of action or behavior.

anomalies Facts or events that deviate from what is normal or expected.

antisemitic Hostile to or prejudiced against Jews.

assassinate To murder someone for a political reason.

biased Unfairly prejudiced for or against someone or something.

Black Death An outbreak of plague in the 1300s that killed a third of the population in Europe.

brainwashed Pressurized into the unthinking acceptance of beliefs very different from one's original beliefs.

climate change A change in regional and global climates that most experts attribute to carbon dioxide released into the atmosphere by burning fossil fuels such as coal and oil.

collude To come to a secret understanding.

conspiracy A secret plan by a group of people to do something unlawful or harmful.

conspiracy theories Beliefs that secret but powerful organizations are responsible for unexplained events.

embargo An official ban on trade with a particular country.

fundamentalist Someone who believes in a strict, literal form of a religion.

greenhouse gases Gases released into the atmosphere by human activity that trap heat, raising temperatures on Earth.

hackers Criminals who access computer systems without authority.

Holocaust The name given to a Nazi plan to wipe out Europe's Jews and other victims during World War II.

impeach To charge the holder of a public office with malpractice.

inflation A rapid rise in prices.

insider trading Trading on the stock market based on illegal access to confidential information.

paparazzi Photographers who pursue famous people to take photographs of them to sell.

scrutiny Close observation or examination.

trusts Associations between businesses that set out to have a monopoly in a market.

vaccine A substance made from the agents that cause disease that is injected into the body to provide immunity against disease.

FURTHER RESOURCES

Books

Adamson, Thomas K. *Apollo 11 Moon Landing*. You Choose. North Mankato, MN: Capstone Press, 2016.

Loh-Hagan, Virginia. *Roswell.* Urban Legends: Don't Read Alone! Ann Arbor, MI: Cherry Lake Publishing, 2017.

Mara, Wil. *The Assassination of John F. Kennedy*. Archaeological Mysteries. New York: Franklin Watts, 2015.

Murray, Laura K. *The 9/11 Terror Attacks*. Turning Points. North Mankato, MN: Creative Educational, 2016.

Samuels, Charlie. *Conspiracy!* Mystery Files. New York City: Crabtree Publishing Company, 2013.

Scherer, Lauri S. *Global Warming.* Introducing Issues with Opposing Viewpoints. Detroit: Greenhaven Press, 2012.

Websites

www.bbc.co.uk/science/space/solarsystem/collections/moon_landing_conspiracy_theories
This page from the BBC has evidence showing the moon landing was real.

people.howstuffworks.com/conspiracy-theory.htm
This page from How Stuff Works explains the appeal of conspiracy theories and how they spread.

www.scientificamerican.com/article/why-do-some-people-believe-in-conspiracy-theories/
A Scientific American article that looks at why some people believe in conspiracy theories.

Publisher's note to educators and parents: Our editors have carefully reviewed these websites to ensure that they are suitable for students. Many websites change frequently, however, and we cannot guarantee that a site's future contents will continue to meet our high standards of quality and educational value. Be advised that students should be closely supervised whenever they access the Internet.

INDEX